# I Know Your Name

## Corrie Piersma

BookLeaf
Publishing

India | USA | UK

Presentation by *BookLeaf Publishing*

Web: www.bookleafpub.com

E-mail: info@bookleafpub.com

ISBN: 9789360941291

First edition 2024

*to Caleb - my heart and soul,*

*for always saying yes to me with your
whole heart and*

*for being the safest home I've ever known*

# ACKNOWLEDGEMENT

Endless thanks to endlessly wonderful humans, places and colors.

To Caleb & our quiver, for being a family full of hope and legacy.

To my incredible mother, for teaching me how to love and how to fight.

To my baby sister, for finding me in darkness and holding me while I wrestle.

To Tiara, for challenging me and always advocating for me to fight for creating.

To Mimi and Christine, for your presence that is still felt and always missed.

To my kiddos in Rhino and LIFT, for keeping my eyes glittering full of wonder.

To my wonderful teachers over the years who believed in me and took the time to let me know

-

Mr. Gibson, Ms. Masisak, Mrs. Pooler and Mrs. Anderson.

And to me, for having words and releasing them. You are brave and you are kind, too.

I am who I am because you are all who, how and why you are. Thank you for your encouragement, investment and goodness and for sharing it with me always.

# PREFACE

A letter to YOU -

Howdy-doo ! I can say that because I'm from Kansas and have a degree in Linguistics, so I've earned it. I sincerely appreciate you spending your breath to read that which seems to sweat from my very pores. Each word I read, speak or write is a rich encounter with the world ; I am enamored with words and have been since I can remember.

This book is a gathering of different perspectives, blessings and invitations. It is my hope that every person will feel less alone, more understood and more seen at least once in this book. And hopefully, you'll find a page for your best friend or neighbor - and they'll find a page for their estranged daughter - and so on, until the world is wrought with blistering displays of kindness, compassion and hope.

So while this book might just be 21 short poems, it has much bigger dreams.

May you feel held, heard and seen.

XX,
Corrie

# [thunderclap]

I heard it with my eyes
I saw it even though I wasn't looking
and it made
such a loud sound
I thought I would go blind.

A burst of color so
violent and
vibrant
you could have sworn it was a thunder clap.

And no one else turned to look
because no one heard the sound you didn't make,
the sound you painted so
Vividly
as you rushed
past, just to let me know you were there.

# [a preface]

forever and a day

both, and
all, and
never ending
unceasing
infinity times, no erasies.


we each have our own way
of attempting to
articulate our
infinity.


may the journey of discovery
be another
full and beautiful
eternity.

# [morning]

I dream and dream
and wrestle
and doubt
And morning comes - jarring my reality.

I see you when I sleep
And when I wake it's just a shadow
and morning always comes.

Morning always comes
Morning always comes.
Did you hear ?
Morning always comes.

# [radio silence]

Radio Silence for you
Distraction and chaos for me.

"Sometimes quiet is violent"
And I can't sit with myself for fear of doing or saying
something I'll regret
Can't sit with myself because I can't stand myself
Don't want to look in a mirror
Don't want to eat, couldn't sleep if I wanted to
Or of course,
I'll sleep the day away.

Can't let a pimple be
Can't keep my fingers out of my mouth
Can't stop hitting my head on a wall
Can't stop questioning my every move and word
Pick pick pick
Chew chew chew
Thump thump thump
Why why why ?

And so you've had silence
You've had silence because I cannot hold it, cannot
bear it
And I've run rampant
Looking for things to do, to fix, to be

Searching for anything that isn't myself and the train
wreck of emotions and chemicals and self doubt and
relationships and conflict and
Desperation.

Is anyone there ?
Have you felt what I'm feeling ?
Have you lost your way so deeply and wholly and
severely that it seems impossible to find your way
back and you want to give up, lest fail and find
yourself even deeper ?

I don't wish it on you
And yet I know I need to know solidarity because I
do not think being held will soothe this ache.
And so I'm here. Again. Wondering, wandering,
searching for hope, holding my breath and

Waiting waiting waiting

For the sun to break through
For the storm to still
For my chest to release
For my muscles to relax
For the deep breath.

Just to breathe, just to breathe
And to be okay with the silence
To be okay with me, broken but whole, imperfect but
holy
Good.
Enough.

# [a dreary day]

Today I don't feel like doing anything
I just want to lay in my bed
Don't feel like picking up the phone
I'd say leave a message but I won't listen to it
Because I can't handle another person needing
something from me.

I'm stuck in a rut
My spirit in a noose
And I can't seem to find a light in all of this sunshine
surrounding me.
I promise I'll be fine
But today I'm not sure I can hold it together for you
So please don't ask it of me
Please just let me go
Let me sit in bed all day and feel
All that I must feel
So I can start to heal and continue to grieve
And learn how to be alive and want it
Again

Because today I don't feel like doing anything.
And I'm tired of hauling ass to make it to 8pm
So I can crash again
And wrestle with sleep until the morning
Streams through the windows again
Calling me back into
What feels like suffering.

Terrified to go to sleep
Yet never wanting to get up
It's too much to hold so I've
Detached myself from everyone and
Everything.

It isn't that I don't care
It isn't that I have lost compassion
It isn't that I don't treasure you and us
It's that my hands are tied behind my back
And I'm just trying to hold my head above water.

Someday I hope to hold you close again
But until then
Please be patient with me
Please give me grace
Please don't give up on me.
I'm sorry I've run so far
I'm sorry I've cut you off
I promise it was never my intention,
I just got a little lost.

So I'll wait for you here,
Listening to the leaves rustle on the trees
And crunch beneath my feet
As I breathe once more,
Holding the beast inside
Tight, tight, tighter still.
I will wait for you here.

# [seeking]

So
So I see
So I see you
So I see you've made up your mind.

No church, it's hypocritical
It's tired and judgy, exclusive and cliquey.
No religion, it's stifling
It's brainless, ignorant and brainwashing.

No meat, it's anti-environment
No carbs, they're sugar
No sugar, it's poison

No politics, they're divisive
No masks, they're political
No vaccines, they're toxic
No government, they're corrupt

No gender, it's limiting
No limits, they're confining and confusing and
demeaning and destroying.

I see you, your mind made up
About the world and everyone in it

About the world and everything in it.

And it's good to question, it's good to doubt
It's good to wrestle and disagree
After all, unity without diversity is conformity.

But I see you argue because of the mystery

As if curiosity really did kill the cat
As if exploration was only meant to be planned
down to the moment
As if everything was understandable and
tangible.

I see you argue because you're afraid
You're afraid of being wrong
being rejected
being excluded
being persecuted.

I see you argue because you want to feel
you want to feel alive, feel something at all
you want to feel something more than numbness
something more than emptiness
something more than the razor across your skin
or the dull fog from the medications and drugs.

I get it. I see you. I see the pain, the fear, the
numbness.

I've felt it too.
I've seen the darkest of nights that went on
without a whisper
of dawn –

I'm still here. I am with you.

I see you, your mind made up.

And I see YOU –

I see you looking for answers
looking for hope, for love, for faith
looking for something bigger, something more
something you cannot touch, something you
cannot see.

I SEE you –
not really seeking to find
but seeking to be found.

# [shower song]

Before there were showers
Before there was warm and cold shooting from my
ceiling
There was poetry.
The words that twist and wind
Taking breath after breath to
Bring me to you and you to me.

I won't punch you with my words
I won't tell you much you don't know
But I might tell you what you're afraid to show.


A sweet song of spring
A sorrowful one for fall
The blazing one of summer
And the quietest one of all –

Do you hear it ?

Do you hear the song ?
The words that twist and wind
Like the wind in the trees
Dancing without ceasing
Because it's what they were made to do.
A song without a melody
Still spinning in sweet harmony
A neverending symphony
Full of everything that's sacred

To you and to me.

Oh how I wish it holds you close
And brings me closer still
The words that swirl and twirl
Like colors splashing in my very eyes
Colors that paint me and paint what's in front of me
But it's not just the light I can see
For you can see it too, I'm sure of it.
The words the words the words –
May they never stop rolling
Never stop singing
Never stop dancing
Never stop.

# [tempered]

How strong must a breeze be
To make the branches sway ?
How gentle yet firm must the wind blow
To cause the reeds to bend but not break ?
We can measure its speed, its direction -
Though perhaps not as quickly as it shifts -
But we cannot measure its breath nor breadth
Nor can we comprehend how it dances
With itself
In order to cause
The world
To dance for us.

# [intertwixt]

"Do you like colors today ?" He asked, unassuming.

My spirit somersaults with laughter, like a bubbling spring. How to explain ?

I don't LIKE colors - we are part of each other, Intertwined and intertwixt by our innermost pieces.

Colors are my imaginary friends that everyone else can see, but no one else seems to hear.

So - yes ? I like them today.

# [back home]


A heart revived, a belly full
Eyes that slllllliiiiidddee and flutter between open and
closed
Aching knees and back spasms, tiny trinkets to
remind me of home

And all I can hear are the giggles of two rays of sun
Bubbling and babbling and
 sh ri e k i n g      !

A heart yearning, another whole,
Missing.

No words to capture
     the b l  a  n      k sp a       c
e s
which of course can only currently be filled by
the meeting of expectation and fulfillment.

# [brimming]

So this is what it is
to be touched by heaven
to be overwhelmed by being seen
to the point of brimming over.

I had forgotten what it felt like to be light

And remembered what it is to be held once again.

The close kind of held, where you're warm and
almost can't breathe
but in a good way
because you're so relieved you're floating
higher and higher until the tops of the tallest trees
tickle your toes.
So this is what it is.

footnote :
Still we fight to rebuild
But it seems safe to say
The foundation has set and
The very first brick has been laid.

# [from where I'm standing]

Today feels hard, but not in the density kind of way
Instead, like a million tiny thumb tracks
Stabbed into my eyes, repeatedly
While being forced to watch a bad movie
in a language I don't understand.

I am eating lunch, one dog at my feet and the other
perched in a window
The chicken is so crispy and delicious,
But still I go slowly, taking small bites to make it last.
We're not doing well, financially,
And I worry about keeping food on the table, so I
hoard every meal I eat
Just in case.

I remember different days,
harder in their own right.
18 hour shifts and 3 AM 6-mile bike rides home
in the rain
Working hard to pedal
to go downhill
In the endless gusts of wind.
Uphill both ways
Like our grandparents used to say.

I remember bussing tables
And eating other people's leftovers
Because otherwise I wouldn't consume anything

Excepting the fruit snacks I always kept stocked ;
Priorities and such.


I remember the shame
Coupled with relief
When a friend showed up with groceries
Or ordered a pizza to my house
Just so THEY knew I'd be okay for another few days.


I remember selling
ANYTHING I could
Just to see another day where I wasn't
Fumbling through kitchen cabinets to find something
quick to bring up my blood sugar before I passed out
Because I'd only eaten one cup of steamed vegetables
in three days.


But from where I'm standing, it's easy to see
I'm safe now.
It's easy to see
My tribe has always had my back.


Where I'm standing,
Things are getting better
And better still.


From where I'm standing,
There is hope.


There is hope
Because there has been progress
Because nothing is perfect

Because the chicken is delicious
Because my puppy is warming my feet
Because I'm still breathing.


I've come a long way to belong to myself,
Come home to myself
Treasure and love myself -
So while today is hard,
I know - even if I don't feel -

I can take one breath
and then
I can take one step.

Lather, rinse, repeat.

# [I love you, even when you forget]

It feels like I've lost you, like you're gone even though you're still here.
It looks like you and the voice is the same but it isn't you.
It's a shell of you, like saltless food.

I cry even thinking of calling you, feeling guilty for not doing it more. But you won't remember it anyway.

Will this be the time you forget me ?

None of this is fair, especially not for you.  I'm grateful at least you don't see it's happening anymore – you're lost in it.

I wish I could go back and tell you it'd be okay. I wish someone would come and tell me the same.

It's scary for me, but you're not afraid. Like always, your hands are raised to the sky as you sing praises.

You forget how incredibly loved and cherished you are, but now you can read it again and again and again.

I will love you when you forget my name.
I will love you when you forget yours.
I will love you, forever and for always.

# [a song to the ones in darkness]

I don't need to hear what I know
I don't need your prayers
I don't want to hear it could always be worse
and I certainly don't want your answers.

If only I could tell you
the point to this pain -
the suffering and endless cycles
of writhing screams and inarticulable reasons

If only I could tell you. But I can't.

So instead, I offer you a new song
to let you know you're not alone
to let you know it's not over
and to let you know, I'm in your corner even if no one
else is.

.....

Living with depression doesn't disqualify you.
Living with depression doesn't mean you aren't
strong [enough].
Living with depression doesn't mean you've failed.

If anything, it means your character is powerful
enough to endure hell on earth.

If anything, it means you are resilient and faithful.
If anything, it means you carry the banner of hope.

Because you're still here.
Because you stayed.
Because there is a spirit of fortitude
living within you that refuses to be snuffed.

And so to you, as you wave your flag of victory :

You're still not alone.
You're still strong enough.
You're still good enough.
You're still held.
You're still loved.
You're still worthy.
You're still new.
You're still seen.
You're still chosen.
You're still here.

And damn, am I glad for that.
It feels a lot less lonely with you around.

# [it's today]

Today as I took the trash to the curb, I rushed to the
end of the road, preparing for my day. Planning for
all things to be done, measuring the potential of the
time in front of me with success defined as no
moment wasted, my to-do list miles long, every
moment and breath promised to a task.

As I walked back up, I was
struck
by the giggling of leaves as they watched me
in giddy anticipation
a "we can't wait until she sees" kind of way.

That's when I looked up, instead of down

and I was greeted
by lush green, blue sky and a breeze that
tickled my cheek as a birdsong rang out
high and clear.

My breath
stolen
in a moment of
stillness -
SLAPPED
by the beauty in front of me.

If I'm living in the plan and planning for the future

Then today doesn't matter.
And if today doesn't matter, what does ?

Today is the beginning.

It's a race to
feel and to
be alive and to
stop doing whatever it is you're doing so you
don't miss
what you're becoming.

# [living the dream]

We live in a dream,
Steam rising from patches of sand
Echoing the cries of the skies
Alight from the scorching sun.

We build and we play,
We sew and we pray

A simple life.

Wandering goats
and a shout heard throughout
all of camp
for reconciliation

and unity of all nations.

# [a love note]


Even when I see you across the room

it's like holding sunshine ;
every particle of my
body and
spirit

alive
with light.

# [you used to be]

You used to be my safe place
four strong and sturdy walls
where you would pore into me as you
poured over me
warming me ever-so-gently to my core.

You made me feel clean, made me feel seen –
you were whole and holy,
the place I wrestled with thoughts
and where my faith came to life.

But lately, you're a hellish pit
a mind-bending trap where
I feel berated and shamed
pelted with guilt as each drop from you sears my skin
and tears fly down my face, the sweat mixing with
water.

I avoid you, sitting in my stench, afraid to face you.
I don't want to be reminded of the things I've told
you
the ways I've shared my heart to you
and I can't give be so free and open anymore –
you've ruined that.

Instead of being able to think, you have turned my
mind to be
laser-focused on the things I've lost

the things I've not said
the ways I haven't shown up
As if I needed any help to see the void.

And so now, you are not my safe space,
not a steadfast place of comfort.
You are just a constricting box ; four walls and a
faucet,
no longer my safe space – just a simple (stupid)
shower.

# [we won't have it]

I won't have it.
Generational curses
Over my country, over my people
spun like a noose around
our necks
taut with tension,
threatening the beauty
Purity
Simplicity
of this life
and the truth of light.

I won't have it.
The fatigue that wages war on our very breath
the compounding and the crushing
the dark that feels as if it's coldly seeping into every
part of our soul
the drowning in a desert
the dying of thirst in a world made of water
the aching bones that paralyze you

Lies bringing death and shadow
to a world of abundance and goodness

Loneliness
Suicide
Despair
Fear.

I won't have it.
People believing they're forgotten
Unseen
Unworthy
Ugly
Unheard.

Who told you that ?

Do you know how beautiful you are ?
How beloved you are ?
How fully known you are ?

I will fight for you.
My friends and family
and all who are
scorned, bitter, depressed, lonely, afraid, shamed,
desperate, deceived

I will fight for light, because those curses
they stop here
they end here
and we cry
with gnashing teeth
"No more."

# [wild woman]

They say
"the wilderness is not your home"
And perhaps they are right
But -

I am made of wildness and vibrant, holy light
Talking more with the leaves as they rustle than I do
those of my own species.

The feel of damp earth on the soles of my feet widens
my lungs and rips my heart open to the world around
me - its colors, its song, its habitants.

But wild is not feral.
Wild is uncaged
and untamed
and free.

It is relentless and bold
And it is beautiful.

Footnote :
You decide
where to make your home
and it's okay if others disagree.

It's okay to be different, in fact I would say
our differences are what will

Unite us
Strengthen us
Connect us.

And that's what will change our worlds.

# [I know your name]

I know your name.

Not the way it's spelled or pronounced
Not first, middle, last
Not maiden, not married, no titles or profession -
your name.

To know your name is to know
You.

To know you is to know
Resilience and hope
grace, kindness and freedom.

To know you is to know
a billion different universes -
complex and intricate,
ever-expanding and evolving,
holy and wholly whole.

To know you is to know
the warmth of the sun on my face,
the coolness of the trees in the middle of the forest
and the feel of cold waves upon my naked toes.

To know you
is to know with certainty
that there exists more good in this world
than anything else.

www.ingramcontent.com/pod-product-compliance
Lightning Source LLC
Chambersburg PA
CBHW061729130726
47996CB00006B/2573